The *Grockles'* Guide

An illustrated miscellany of
words and phrases of interest
and use to 'voreigners' in
Somerset

Jeremy Warburg & Tessa Lorant

Published 1985 by The Thorn Press, The Old Vicarage, Godney, Wells, Somerset BA5 1RX.

British Library Cataloguing in Publication Data

Warburg, Jeremy
    The Grockles' (holiday makers') guide: an illustrated miscellany of words and phrases of interest and use to 'voreigners' in Somerset.
    1.   English language — Dialects — England — Somerset —Glossaries, vocabularies, etc.
    I. Title   II. Lorant, Tessa
    427'.38   PE 2032

ISBN 0-906374-23-5
Cover and illustrations by Studio B
Printed by Adams & Sons, Hereford, UK.

CONTENTS

To the people of Somerset.

A Sprig of Holy Thorn (see page 30)

ACKNOWLEDGMENTS

We should like to thank W.G. and Molly Gooden, Rolly and Dorita Hellier and family, Raymond, Queenie and Margaret Hitchcock, Max King, Christopher Stott, Rex Whitcombe, Richard and Diana Wiseman, and the many, many others who, wittingly and unwittingly, have helped us with this book. We alone, of course, are responsible for any defects.

PREFACE

What are **chibbles** - or **jibbles**? What's a **caddy**, or a **joey** or a **squeaker**? What's a **tundish** or a **smeech**? What is **withywind** and what is **withy**? What does it mean to have **the screws**? Does **to go wanting** mean just to go without? Is a **randy** something to do with sex? Is a **truckle** a small truck? What's a **rhine**, or a **crooger**? Who - or what, perhaps - is **Harry**? Who is **Laurence**, and what does it mean to have him on one's back? Is **hunting** cattle the same as hunting foxes? Is **lardy cat** the same as lardy cake? Is a **beetle** (or a **bittle**) just an insect? Is a **chump** just a silly sort of person? Is a **cheese** just food?

You'll find the answers in this book.

For this is a book of words and phrases used in, and in various ways characteristic of, Somerset - in particular of Central Somerset, the Somerset of Avalon and Sedgemoor. And these are some of the words and phrases which the book contains.

They belong to a vocabulary drawn on by many of the people of Somerset. In so far as this is part of regional dialect - and we should make quite clear that we've included other words and phrases, mostly from characteristic occupations such as farming, which we thought would be of interest too - its use has certainly declined: radio and TV, railways, cars and aeroplanes, longer stints at school, and the pressures to conform, have seen to that. But it is still considerable, above all among the older, and especially the male, country folk. They use it mostly when they're talking among them-selves...with family, with friends, and with other local folk. When they're talking to 'foreigners' (**voreigners:** more or less anyone born outside the region) they may well modify their speech and adopt, wherever possible, the words and phrases

5

of the wider community - Standard English forms. They are, to that extent at least, bilingual.

Nonetheless we felt that such a glossary, however incomplete - and we make no claim to completeness - would be interesting, instructive and pleasurable to **voreigners**. (Notice, for instance, the number and variety of terms for clumsiness, and in particular for manual clumsiness, something which obviously matters to communities where so much work is done with the hands.) We felt it would be especially interesting to **grockles** - holidaying 'voreigners', whether from overseas or closer to - even if they didn't often hear these words and phrases used. And we felt that it might possibly be helpful when they did...to know what **purdle, croupy down, dimsey dark, chammering** or **scammish-handed** mean.

Of course they might still have some trouble with the grammar or, more likely, with the way in which words and phrases are pronounced. (We were once completely baffled by the use of **sturs**. It turned out that the speaker was referring to some steers, that is bullocks, in a nearby field.) But, apart from the little that we say about this here, that is a matter for another, larger and more complicated book.

We also felt that this glossary would be of interest and give pleasure to the people of Somerset themselves, in particular perhaps to those who most use the specifically regional words and phrases which form so large a part of the book. Some of them are inclined to be diffident, deprecating, even apologetic, about their dialect. Such an attitude is misconceived. It is misconceived whether or not Somerset dialect is the remains of the court language of King Alfred, as has in fact been claimed. It is misconceived quite simply because language is good, and in no way 'improper' or 'inferior', if it works. So, using it aptly, Somerset folk should delight in the richness and variety of theirs.

And let grockles delight in it as well!

January, 1985.

6

ABIDE: to tolerate, to bear, to put up with. "I can't abide 'em."

ABEAR: as ABIDE.

ACCORDING: dependent on. "That's according..." (i.e. That depends...)

AFEARD: afraid.

AFORE: before.

AFTERCUT: grass that grows after the cut made for hay. Also AFTERGRASS, HE-GRASS, YEAR GRASS.

AFTERGRASS: as AFTERCUT.

AGIN: against - "Put thik (that) ladder agin the wall"; near, beside; by the time that. Also 'GIN.

AH: roughly, but only roughly, synonymous with YES. In fact the use of AH involves at times a somewhat guarded, even reluctant or grudging, attitude to affirmation. Sometimes it just means 'maybe'.

ANCHOR: to dawdle, to potter. Also ANGLE, CADDLE, DIDDLE, DODDLE.

ANGLE: to dawdle, to potter. "I just been angling about the place." Also ANCHOR, CADDLE, DIDDLE, DODDLE.

ANYWHEN: any time. "Anywhen to suit you." See SOMEWHEN.

APS: a boil or purulent spot. Also APSY. Compare Standard English ABSCESS.

APSY: as APS.

ARGATIVE: argumentative. "He's very argative."

ARGIFY: to argue, to dispute.

Reynard (see page 44)

ASHEN FAGGOT: see FAGGOT.

ATHIRT: across. "Let's go athirt there."

BACHE: a slope, rise or small hill – essentially a higher area. We have not come across its use in everyday speech to mean 'a stream, a valley', but the term is quite common in place names and such features of the landscape may also be involved in these. Also BATCH. And see EMMET, KNAP.

BACKALONG: some time ago – "That were backalong"; homewards – "I'll be doddling backalong".

BACK-HANDED: left-handed. Also CACK-HANDED, LEFT-HANDED, SCAMMISH-HANDED, SCRAMMY-HANDED. We have also found BACK-HANDED used for wrong-handed (that is, using the wrong hand in a particular case) and therefore clumsy or awkward with the hands. Also CACK-HANDED, CLUMBLEFISTED, GAMMY-HANDED, HOMICKY, LEFT-HANDED, MUZZLE-HANDED, SCAMMISH-HANDED, SCRAMMY-HANDED. See BACK-HANDER.

BACK-HANDER: a dirty trick, a crooked or deceitful thing to do, something (wrong) done behind one's back. "You've done a b..... back-hander on me." Possibly connected with BACK-HANDED (above) and also with CACK and CACK-HANDED (below).

BAD-ABED: ill enough to be confined to bed.

9

BARTON: a farmyard. The term is comparatively rare now (except in place names), but some (usually middle aged or elderly) people still use it. See MOW-BARTON, RICK-BARTON.

BATCH: as BACHE.

BAWKER: a whetstone. WHETSTONE is also used.

BEASTS: cattle.

BEATER (sometimes pronounced BI-ARTER): a very long-handled implement with a long, straight, relatively light blade set at an acute angle to the handle; it is used for trimming the sides of river banks and rhines, etc - see RHINE.

BEETLE: not only for the insect but for a hefty (two-handed) 'mallet', the head bound with an iron ring. It is used for driving in fence posts, or driving iron wedges into timber to split it, etc. After prolonged use, the wood at the head will fray and turn back on the ring; this has given rise to the expression BEETLE-BROWED. Also BROM-BEETLE, MAUL. And see BONKER. MALLET, which is also used, refers to the smaller, lighter, all-wooden implement used in carpentry.

BENDS: In Elworthy's **West Somerset Word-Book,** 1888, these are defined as 'ridges in land which has been thrown up into "ridge and furrow"', but we have only found it used to refer to relatively flat areas of land between dips or ridges.

BENNET: stiff, coarse grass; old dry stalks of grass. An earlier form of BENT.

BIDE: to stay -"Come roun' an' bide wi' I"; to stay the same - "Wouldn't it be nice if it'd bide like that?".

BIGETY: stuck up, high and mighty.

BILLHOOK (often pronounced BILLUK): a short-handled implement, with a short, thick, heavy, slightly hooked blade; it is used for cutting wood, in layering hedges, etc.

BIRD'S EYE: the wild flower Germander Speedwell, that is Veronica Chamaedrys.

BLOWER: an attack of irritation, irritability. "'E's got a blower on 'im."

BONKER: a cylindrical implement, made of iron, which fits round a stake and is used, by two people, to bonk/drive the stake in.

BOY: not only for a young male but as a friendly, or sometimes derogatory, term for a man.

BRIZE: to bring pressure to bear on, in pushing down, lifting off, opening up, etc. "I'm goin' to brize down on thik (that)." Compare Standard English PRISE or PRIZE. ·

BROM-BEETLE: as BEETLE.

BULLING: of a cow on heat, ready to be served by a bull: the animal is consequently restless and agitated, bellows, and will climb on, and be climbed on by, others.

BURN-BAKE: turf-ash, the mix of soil and ash left after burning the surface of a field to improve its fertility; bonfire-ash.

BURRY: a group of interconnecting rabbit holes. In other words a form of BURROW, but the pronunciation might baffle one.

CACK: excrement.

CACK-HANDED: left-handed - also BACK-HANDED, LEFT-HANDED, SCAMMISH-HANDED, SCRAMMY-HANDED; clumsy or awkward with the hands - also BACK-HANDED, CLUMBLEFISTED, GAMMY-HANDED, HOMICKY, LEFT-HANDED, MUZZLE-HANDED, SCAMMISH-HANDED, SCRAMMY-HANDED.

CADDLE: a muddle or difficulty. "I'm in a proper caddle". We have also found it used as a verb meaning to dawdle, to potter - also ANCHOR, ANGLE, DIDDLE, DODDLE.

CADDY: the runt in a litter of pigs. Also CADMAN, CAGMAN, JOEY, SQUEAKER.

CADMAN: this is used, though less frequently than CADDY or JOEY, to refer to the runt in a litter of pigs. Also CAGMAN.

CAGMAN: as CADMAN.

CATCH HEAT: to get warm with exercise.

CAUL, CAUL FAT: the fat covering the intestines of a pig and used for 'bundling up' faggots - see FAGGOT. The fat is membraneous, looking like a net or veil, and it's interesting to note that CAUL, in Standard English, refers to a net or covering for the head and to the membrane covering the head of some infants at birth. It is presumably connected with COWL, a cap or hood such as monks wear. See KETCHER.

CAVINGS: chaff. Also HUSKS, SHAVINGS.

CHAM: to chew; to eat (to chew) noisily - also CHAMMER.

CHAMMER: to eat (to chew) noisily - also CHAM; a noisy eater. CHAMMER is also used (the connection is obvious) to mean to chatter, to talk a lot, to gossip - see YOP; and a CHAMMER, in this context, is one who does this - also CHATTERBAG, NAGGAR, NEWSBAG, RAGBAG, WINDBAG, and see YOPPER (under YOP).

CHATTERBAG: a gossip. Also CHAMMER, NAGGAR, NEWSBAG, RAGBAG, WINDBAG.

CHEDDARING: no, not going to Cheddar, that well-known Somerset town, nor even eating some of the famous cheese named after it, but "the orderly piling of curds into masses" in the cheese making process. (Patrick Rance, **The Great British Cheese Book**, 1982.)

CHEDDY: like the more general SPUD, TATER, a potato. Also CHITTY, TATY, TEDDY, TIDDY.

CHEESE: not only the food but, in cider making, the layered stack of ground apples and binder made, or 'put up', on the press, and from which the juice is extracted. See LISSOM, POMACE.

13

CHIBBLES: young onions with the green stalk attached; spring onions. Also JIBBLES.

CHILVER: a ewe lamb. CHILVER is also used to refer to a condition which involves the swelling of the udders (the swelling will sometimes extend into the perineal region) of, primarily, dairy cattle, and in particular heifers. This condition may occur just before calving, and results from the animal eating too well. Incidentally, it occurs less in West Somerset because the pasture there is less rich.

CHITTERLINGS: the smaller intestines of a pig or other edible animal. Boiled or fried, hot or cold, with salt and mustard or sprinkled with vinegar, this is an economical dish still enjoyed in, though by no means restricted to, Somerset; but it is now much less popular and less inexpensive than before. It is one of several dishes made with the obscurer parts of pigs, of which animals it used, at any rate, to be said that nothing was wasted but the squeak.

CHITTY: potato. Also CHEDDY, TATY, TEDDY, TIDDY. CHITTING, incidentally, is in general use as a gardening term which refers to the process of 'sprouting' potatoes before planting them out.

CHOOKY, CHOOKY PIG: a pig. The terms are associated with children's language.

CHUMP: a chunk, or log, of (fire)wood.

CLIDER: goosegrass, Galium Aparine. No doubt related to CLEAVERS, a name for this plant in quite general use. Incidentally, goosegrass is so called because its tender shoots make good eating for goslings. Also SWEETHEARTS.

14

CLOTTED CREAM: the cream (the oily part of the milk) taken from scalded milk is called CLOT-TED cream because it forms clots or 'clouts' on the surface of the milk. Also known as Somersetshire or Devonshire cream. Mrs Beeton's recipe may be of interest: Allow the milk to stand 24 hours in winter, and half that time when the weather is warm. Set the milkpan on a stove and allow the milk to become hot, but do not boil. The cream will be clotted when the undulations on the surface look thick, and small rings appear. The time taken depends on the size of the pan and the heat of the fire, but the slower it is done the better. The cream should be taken to the dairy when it is sufficiently scalded, and skimmed the next day... Perhaps we should add that it is of course simpler to go to any good Somerset dairy or other stockist and buy your clotted cream!

CLUMBERSOME: clumsy, awkward. Also GAMMY, SCAMMISH.

CLUMBLEFISTED: clumsy or awkward with the hands. Also BACK-HANDED, CACK-HANDED, GAMMY-HANDED, HOMICKY, LEFT-HANDED, MUZZLE-HANDED, SCAMMISH-HANDED, SCRAMMY-HANDED. This is obviously something which matters in communities where so much work is done with the hands.

COCK: a small heap of hay, a haycock. This usage is comparatively rare now and is often thought of as outmoded, since, with sophisticated haymaking machinery available, such heaps are not much made. To COCK IT UP means, in this context, to make such a heap. Also POOK.

CODGER: to do something, or somebody who does something, in a makeshift way. (AN OLD CODGER is perhaps one who, owing to age, can only manage to do things in such a makeshift way.)

COMICAL: difficult, bad-tempered or odd. "He's a comical ol' b....."

COMBE (pronounced COOM): a deep hollow or valley in a hillside. A constituent of many place names. Also COOMBE.

CONEY: a (wild) rabbit.

COOMBE: as COMBE.

COOPY, COOPY HEN: a hen. The terms are associated with children's language.

Dillies (see page 18)

COUCH (sometimes pronounced COOCH): not only for the grass which is a tiresome and prolific weed, but, as a verb, to settle down or sit. See QUAT. Someone who is IN COUCH is settled down, on their backside, etc.

COUPY DOWN (pronounced COOPY DOWN): as (the more usual) CROUPY DOWN.

COW PLAT: cow dung.

CRANE: a heron. Herons frequent, for example, the moors - see MOOR - and are almost always referred to as CRANES, which don't. HERON (roughly) may well refer to herring.

CREATURE: a woman or girl, never a man or boy. (The usage is derogatory and belongs to the male-chauvinist age). Also used to refer to a bug or insect, presumably of either sex.

CROOJER: a woodlouse - also GRAMFER and GRAMFER-CROOJER; one who hides away in a corner, as a woodlouse 'hides' under wood.

CROUPY DOWN (pronounced CROOPY DOWN): to crouch; to get down, as one may under a hedge or fence. Also (less often) COUPY DOWN. Compare Standard English CROUCH, CREEP, STOOP.

CROWDIE: like CRUMBLE, a pudding made with fruit, most often apple, covered with a layer of pastry at the 'crumb' stage, and then baked.

CURRANTS: not only the fruits, fresh or dried, but droppings such as sheep's or rabbits' which somewhat resemble them. See TRUCKLES.

CUT: to castrate, by using a surgical knife to cut the cords, and remove the testicles, of a horse, pig, older calf... See PINCH, RING.

17

DADDOCKY: rotten (especially of wood).

DAMN THEE ARE: signifying (usually emphatic) agreement; yes. See AH.

DAP: to bounce (a ball); also to go quickly - "I'm just goin' to dap down town".

DAPS: image of, as in "He's the daps of his Mum". The word is also used to refer to plimsolls - "I got to gi' miself some daps". PLIMSOLLS is considered posh.

DEDDICKIE: a gipsy. GIPSY and TRAVELLER are also (and now more often) used. Also DEDDICKOY.

DEDDICKOY: as DEDDICKIE.

DIDDLE: to dawdle, to potter. Also ANCHOR, ANGLE, CADDLE, DODDLE.

DILLY, DILLY DUCK: a duck. "We ought to be down there looking for some dillies." The terms are associated with children's language.

DIMSEY, DIMSEY DARK: twilight, dusk; murky. "It's getting dimsey." Also DUMCEY, DUMCEY DARK.

DITCH: a fast flowing, narrow water channel cut out of low-lying land to drain away excess water. The term is also used (from a technical viewpoint, wrongly) of small rhines. See RHINE, DRAIN.

DODDLE: to dawdle, to potter. Also ANCHOR, ANGLE, CADDLE, DIDDLE.

Cranes (see page 17)

DOUBLETEETH: molar teeth. Also GNASHERS, GRINDERS.

DOUT: to extinguish, put out. "Dout they lights", "Dout thik (that) fire".

DOWNALONG: along, towards or near - all in a generally downward direction from where one is. "Thee go downalong thik (that) ditch, thee go upalong", but also "It's downalong Shapwick". See UPALONG.

DRAIN: not only the domestic pipe for draining waste water but also the substantial, man-made, cross-country channel (not, like a canal, for transport) accepting water from the smaller, land-draining ditches and rhines. Drains may be relatively small, say ten feet across when several miles inland, but become very substantial nearer to the sea. At high water time they must be able to carry, sometimes to store, very large amounts of water from the lowlands. This gives the rivers a chance to drain their waters into the sea. The considerable flooding of the lowlands, which used to be a feature of the winter landscape (and, in wet seasons, of the summer's too), is becoming rare as more and more drainage channels are dug out. See DITCH, RHINE.

DRANG: a passageway between buildings, an alley. "I went down through drang."

DRECKLY: directly. A matter of pronunciation, but one could be misled. At any rate it often means 'soon'.

DROVE: a track or path, especially one along which cattle, or other animals, are driven. To DROVE involves 'driving' the animals along such tracks. See HUNT.

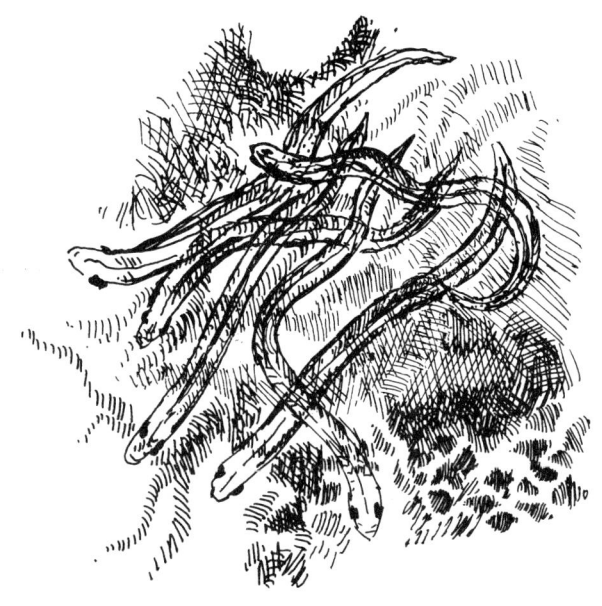

Elvers (see page 22)

DUMCEY, DUMCEY DARK: dusk, twilight; murky. Also DIMSEY, DIMSEY DARK.

DUNCH: dim-witted, unable to learn. "He were always a dunch lad at school." Presumably connected with DUNCE. Also used to refer to the bluntness of an implement.

DUNCHED, DUNCHED UP: cramped. "We're all dunched up in here". It can also mean worked up, tense.

DUNGFORK: a fork used for shifting dung, though not only dung.

DURNS: the frame of a door; a doorway.

21

EARLY WIGS: earwigs.

ELVER: Standard English, but not, perhaps, at all well-known, it means a young eel, and in Somerset usually refers to one the size of a fine straw roughly three inches long. Cooked, these are considered a great delicacy by many folk.

EMMET: an ant; a little fly. Thus an EMMET-BATCH is an ant-hill - see BACHE, BATCH. We have also found EMMETS used occasionally to refer to holiday makers or tourists, especially where these are found in large throngs or teeming trails. See GROCKLE.

EMPT: to empty.

EUCHERED: tired out - also KNOOKERED, LAGGED OUT. The word is also used to refer to being stuck, as in a problem.

EVERY WHIP'S WHILE: occasionally, now and then, i.e. the time between the strokes of a whip.

Bear in mind that f is often pronounced as **v**.

FADDY: (as slang PADDY) bad temper. To be IN A FADDY is to be in a temper. Also STEWER.

FAGGOT: not only a term of abuse applied to a woman - "You silly old faggot" - but used in the (Somerset and Devon) expression ASHEN FAG-GOT: a bundle of ash wood bound with thongs and burned as part of an old Yule-tide custom which still persists, at least in Curry Rivel, where it is observed on January 5th, 'old' Christmas Eve. (The custom is briefly described and discussed in M. Walker, **Old Somerset Customs**, 1984.) FAG-GOT is also used to refer to a particular, rela-tively inexpensive food, not of course by any means restricted to Somerset but certainly still popular in it: a bundle, in this case a small ball, consisting of pig's liver, and maybe lights and melt - see MELT - often mixed with breadcrumbs and seasoned. The bundle is 'done up' with caul fat - see CAUL.

FAIRING: not only the windscreen on a motor-bike, but small cakes (gingerbread, brandysnaps) sold at fairs.

FALLING ABROAD: getting stout, running to fat; falling to pieces.

FLICK: the fat surrounding the kidneys of pigs. It may be melted down for lard or attached to and used for basting pork roasts, say, or turkey.

FLUMP: to flop down.

FOREIGNER: not only used of those born outside the United Kingdom, but, essentially, of anyone born outside the 'old' county of Somerset – though a residence of, say, twenty and more years evidently makes one less 'foreign' than one was, and certainly not a holiday maker or tourist – see GROCKLE. Also VOREIGNER.

FORESPUR: a hock of pork.

A Holy Thorn (see page 30)

G

GAFFER: like the more general BOSS, a person in authority. See SQUIRE.

GAMMY: clumsy, awkward - also CLUMBER-SOME, SCAMMISH; in some way physically defective, as a GAMMY leg, which may well involve awkwardness, etc.

GAMMY-HANDED: clumsy or awkward with the hands. Also BACK-HANDED, CACK-HANDED, CLUMBLEFISTED, HOMICKY, LEFT-HANDED, MUZZLE-HANDED, SCAMMISH-HANDED, SCRAMMY-HANDED.

GATCHEL: the mouth.

GEEK: to look fixedly at, to stare. Also GLAZE.

GERT: large, great. Often used in conjunction with BIG. A GERT GATCHEL, or a GERT BIG GATCHEL, refer to a big mouth, often in the sense of loud or boastful.

'GIN: against; near, beside; by the time that -"I'll have that done 'gin you come back." Also AGIN.

GLASTONBURY THORN: Crataegus Monogyna Praecox, a variant of the native hawthorn, and famous for flowering at Christmas. A flowering spray is cut every year from the tree outside St John's Church, in Glastonbury, and sent to the Queen. Also known as – and see – HOLY THORN.

Glastonbury Tor

GLASTONBURY TOR: see TOR.

GLAZE: to stare. Also GEEK.

GNASHERS: molar teeth – also DOUBLETEETH, GRINDERS; also used of teeth generally, including false teeth.

GO BACK: to diminish or change direction (as the wind does); to deteriorate or fail in health.

GOUT: an outside drain. "Tip it down the gout hole."

GRAMFER: commonly used for grandfather, and for an elderly man - also GRAMPS. It is also used to refer to the crane-fly (daddy longlegs) - also GRAMFER-LONGLEGS; and to the woodlouse - also GRAMFER-CROOJER, CROOJER.

GRAMFER-CROOJER: the woodlouse. Also CROOJER, GRAMFER.

GRAMFER-LONGLEGS: the crane-fly (daddy longlegs).

GRAMPS: a grandfather or elderly man. Also GRAMFER.

GRINDERS: molar teeth. Also DOUBLETEETH, GNASHERS.

GRIPE: to make a channel to drain off surface water. "I'm going griping 'day down moor" (today down on the moor). Also used of the channel itself.

GROCKLE: West Country word for a holiday maker or tourist. See EMMET.

GROUNDS: fields; cultivated land. See PLOUGH-GROUNDS.

GUDDLE: to eat or drink fast or voraciously - compare Standard English GUZZLE. The colloquial GOLLOP is also used.

27

Bear in mind that h is often 'dropped'.

HACK: to make a mess of; a mess - "He's making a hack of it." Also HACKLE, and see CODGER. HACK is also used to refer to a cough and to coughing. Also HACKLE, and see HUSK.

HACKLE: as HACK.

HANDPAT: near at hand; easy to do (because near at hand) - "You've got it handpat."

HAPS: the latch of a gate or door; to latch a gate or door. Compare Standard English HASP.

HARRY: the devil. Also OLD HARRY. HARRY is also used to refer to an adder or to a grass snake. See VIPER.

HEAVE: to sweat, as of flagstones, pavements, and so on, in oppressive weather; to be crowded (close) with people. Also in the sense of raise and thus, FROST HEAVE, the raising of soil by frost. HEAVY (pronounced HEEVY) is used of oppressive, damp, sweaty, uncomfortable or crowded conditions. A place subject to such conditions may be referred to as HEAVED (HEEVED) OUT.

HEEVY: see HEAVE.

HEFT: to lift. "Just help me heft this up."

Somerset Basket-maker (see Withy, page 60)

29

HE-GRASS: grass that grows after the cut made for hay. Also AFTERCUT, AFTERGRASS, YEAR GRASS.

HINGE: the heart, liver and lights of a pig, calf, sheep. "I'll 'ave thik (that) 'inge."

HOLY THORN: Crataegus Monogyna Praecox, a variant of the native hawthorn. The tree is unusual in that it blooms in winter, bursting into green leaf and flower, with the summer scent of May, at any time from November onwards, usually carrying both flower and fruit at the same time. Many legends are associated with the Holy Thorn, and there are a variety of possible reasons for its being called Holy, some of which are discussed in D. Hawkins, **Avalon and Sedgemoor**, 1973.

HOMEGROUND: the field nearest to the farmhouse. See GROUNDS.

HOMICKY: clumsy or awkward with the hands. Also BACK-HANDED, CACK-HANDED, CLUMBLEFISTED, GAMMY-HANDED, LEFT-HANDED, MUZZLE-HANDED, SCAMMISH-HANDED, SCRAMMY-HANDED.

HOP: bits of wood in a fire may HOP, that is hop about, fly. See SPARK.

HUNT: with reference to cattle, to walk them from one place to another. See DROVE.

HUSK: a (hoarse, husky) cough; to cough (hoarsely). HUSK in younger cattle is a condition caused by lungworms and is fatal if not treated soon. See HACK, HACKLE.

HUSKS: chaff. Also CAVINGS, SHAVINGS.

J

JAR: to jam or fix (for example a door or window).

JIBBER: a restless horse, one which jibs or baulks at going ahead; someone who is fearful or wary of doing something.

JIBBLES: young onions with the green stalk attached; spring onions. Also CHIBBLES.

JOEY: the runt in a litter of pigs. Also CADDY, CADMAN, CAGMAN, SQUEAKER.

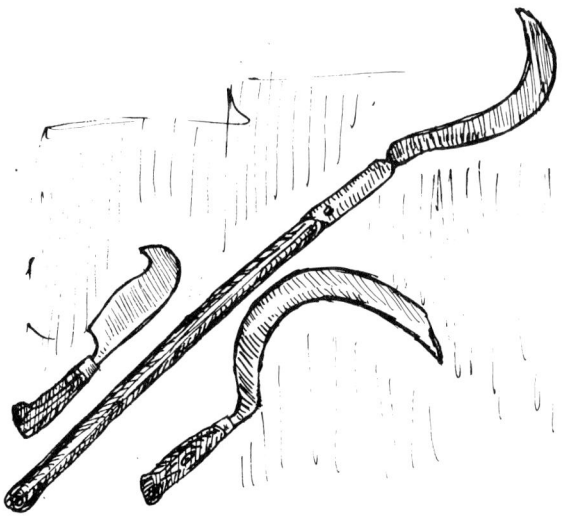

Billhook, Staffhook and Reaphook
(see pages 11, 52 & 44)

KETCHER: the fat covering the intestines of a pig, and used for 'wrapping up' faggots - see FAGGOT. Also CAUL, CAUL FAT.

KNAP: a small rise or hillock. See BACHE.

KNOOKERED: tired out, exhausted. Presumably related to KNACKERED. Also EUCHERED, LAGGED OUT.

A Want (see page 59)

L

LAGGED OUT: tired out, exhausted. Also EUCHERED, KNOOKERED.

LARDY CAT: sometimes of a ginger-coloured cat. We have also found it used as a variant of LARDY CAKE. This dough cake, which takes its name from the pats of fat, originally 'lard', dabbed on the rolled out surface, is very popular in Somerset, though not of course by any means restricted to it, and is to be found in many local bakeries. It is often referred to simply as LARDY. "I'll have some lardy, please."

LAURENCE: a south-western sprite associated with idleness. So, "He's got Laurence about him" or "She's on the Laurence" means that he or she is being lazy, indolent and so on. It is also used to refer to irritability; thus "He's got Laurence on his back" may be used to mean 'He's irritable' - possibly because 'he' wants to be lazy and someone is trying to get 'him' to do something!

LEARY: hungry; tired with hunger; thin; empty (usually of the stomach, but a trailer or carrier, for example, may be leary - that is, empty - too).

LEFT-HANDED: as commonly used, referring to one who is predisposed to use the left rather than the right hand – also BACK-HANDED, CACK-HANDED, SCAMMISH-HANDED, SCRAMMY-HANDED; but also used to refer to clumsiness or awkwardness with the hands – also BACK-HANDED, CACK-HANDED, CLUMBLEFISTED, GAMMY-HANDED, HOMICKY, MUZZLE-HANDED, SCAMMISH-HANDED, SCRAMMY-HANDED.

LEVELS: as in Somerset Levels, the lowlands which stretch across the Central Somerset plain. Not actually level, of course, but Glastonbury Tor, which is no great hill – see TOR – is a landmark for miles, which shows how flat the land really is. See MOOR.

LIPPERY: showery, in-and-out weather.

LISSOM: one of the layers of ground apples and binder in a cheese 'put up' to make cider. See CHEESE, POMACE.

LONGDOG: a greyhound, presumably because of the length of the body and legs in relation to the total size. So, QUICK AS A LONGDOG (or LONGDON and LONGDONG, where the speaker is unaware of the connection with greyhound and simply means fast), RUN LIKE A LONGDOG.

LOVING-IDOL: a particular friend; a favourite.

LUNCH: sometimes used of a mid-morning snack – elevenses – the midday meal being very much more often referred to as DINNER.

M

MAIN: very; great.

MAUL: a hefty, two handed 'mallet', the head bound with an iron ring, used for driving in fence posts or for driving iron wedges into timber to split it, and so on. Also BEETLE, BROM-BEETLE. And see BONKER.

MELT: a mammal's spleen, and, in the case of a pig's, fried to make an inexpensive dish considered a delicacy by some.

MIND: remember. "I mind when the selfsame dresses were about four and eleven."

MOOR: not elevated pastures but, here, low-lying, often marshy grass- and pastureland. The moors are edged with man-made rhines and ditches to drain the land - see DITCH, RHINE. The Somerset equivalent of the East Anglian fens is peatmoor - marshy land in which peat is being formed beneath the surface - but this forms only part of the lowlands. See LEVELS.

MOOT: the stump and roots of a tree. See MORE.

MORE: the root or roots of a tree. From the German for carrot. See MOOT.

MOW-BARTON: still occasionally used, and referring to the farmyard where the mows (stacks of corn, hay) used to be, but are now very rarely, kept. See BARTON.

MUGGET: the intestines of a young heifer or sheep.

MUMP: the peat industry is still - though for how much longer? - substantial in Central Somerset. But, now that a great deal of the work previously done by hand has been taken over by machines, many of the traditional peat-terms are no longer in use and those that remain are not necessarily used in quite the old way. However, where peat is still dug by hand - which is rare now - the term MUMP may be used to refer to a block of peat dug out in this way.

MUZZLE-HANDED: clumsy or awkward with the hands. Also BACK-HANDED, CACK-HANDED, CLUMBLEFISTED, GAMMY-HANDED, HOMICKY, LEFT-HANDED, SCAMMISH-HANDED, SCRAMMY-HANDED.

Longdogs (see page 34)

NAGGAR: a gossip. Also CHAMMER, CHATTERBAG, NEWSBAG, RAGBAG, WINDBAG.

NEWSBAG: as NAGGAR.

NIT: nor (yet). "I ain't got no smokes, nit no money to get 'em."

A Coney (see page 16)

O

OLD HARRY: the devil. Also **HARRY**.

Withies (see page 60)

PARROCK: a paddock.

PICK: a two, three or four pronged fork for general use on a farm.

PIGSCHOPS: antirrhinums, snapdragons. So called, presumably, because of the flower's resemblance to the mouth and jaws of a pig. (In fact the word is also used to refer to that part of a human face.) ANTIRRHINUM means, literally, opposite the nose. And, incidentally, SNAPDRAGON is so called because the lower lip of the plant's corolla, when parted, snaps shut 'like a dragon's jaw'.

PINCH: to castrate (young calves, sheep) by using pincers designed to 'pinch' the cords, which then wither. See CUT, RING.

PISSABED: a dandelion. The plant has diuretic properties. Compare French PISSENLIT. Note, incidentally, that French DENT DE LION (dandelion) means literally tooth of lion, and the leaves of the plant do have jagged, tooth-like edges.

PITCH: to settle, as snow when it settles and remains on the ground. Ground which has PITCHED OFF has dried out and firmed after being wet.

PLIM: to swell, increase in size, as a door swells with damp or a barrel swells when soaked.

PLOUGH-GROUNDS: tilled fields; arable land. See GROUNDS.

POG: to poke at with the fist; to push.

POKED IN: people who are merely standing or sitting nearby and not causing a nuisance may be described as POKED IN - "What are they poked in there for?" - but there is usually the sense that they have pushed or thrust themselves in and may well be in the way: "They were poked in in front of us."

A Rhine (see page 44)

POMACE: in cider making, the dry apple pulp remaining after the juice has been extracted from a cheese - see CHEESE. This residue is either thrown away or fed to stock.

POOK: a small heap of hay. The word is not much used now and is generally thought of as outmoded, since, with sophisticated haymaking machinery available, such heaps are not much made. To POOK IT UP means to make such a heap. Also COCK.

POPS: sweets. A word associated with the language of children.

PRICKER: a Y-shaped stick which may be stuck in the ground to pin down a piece of a hedge when layering it.

PUGGLED: daft, stupid; also, like SKIMMISHED, drunk.

PURDLE: to cause to fall over or spin round and round. For example, "We purdled 'ee over", of shooting a fox. To PURDLE ALONG is to go at a good rate.

PURT: neat - "That's a purt job"; pretty; bright, i.e. intelligent. Also PURTY.

PURTY: as PURT.

PUTT: a heavy, two-wheeled tip-cart. From the pots, balanced on a horse's back, in which manure used to be carried to the fields. The cart which took on the same job took on the same name. But, since such carts are outmoded now, so, generally, is the use of the word, though we have heard of its use to refer to, for example, a two or three ton trailer!

QUAT: to squat or sit. See COUCH, SQUAT. QUAT is also used of a place where, for example, a hare, rabbit or pheasant squats, sits tight, etc.

QUIRK: to moan, whine or complain.

QUIST: a wood pigeon. Also WOOD QUIST. But the term is now thought of as 'old'.

Quists (see page 42)

RAFTY: rancid, 'off', bad-tasting (applied to bacon, for example). We have also come across the use of the word to mean crafty.

RAGBAG: a (usually female) gossip. See CHAM-MER, CHATTERBAG, NAGGAR, NEWSBAG, WINDBAG. RAGBAG is also used to refer to an untidy woman, and to a tramp.

RANDY: a party, merry-making, jollification, lark about. To be or go ON THE RANDY is to enjoy one-self, in other words,to merrymake. We have also come across the expression used to refer to play-ing truant, presumably on the basis that in doing so one is likely to be merrier than before one went.

RANGLE: to twine or twist about, in the manner of a climbing plant; that which twists and turns. "What a b..... rangle all up through 'ere." To RANGLE is also used to mean to take a long time to decide.

RAYBALLING: fishing for eels with a bunch, or ball, of worms fixed on a pole. A long established practice; it is mentioned, for example, in Jennings' **Somerset Dialect**, 1825, and no doubt existed long before.

REAPHOOK (often pronounced RIPPUK): short-handled implement with a long, curved blade – a large sickle – used for cutting grass, rushes, brushwood, hedges.

REDLEGS: a common word for the weed Polygonum Persicaria. See REDSHANK.

REDSHANK: a common word for the weed Polygonum Persicaria. Posher than REDLEGS (above).

REYNARD: a fox. "Look at reynard thar." This has a long and distinguished ancestry, going back to the name of the fox in the celebrated beast epic of Low German origin, Reynard the Fox. The word derives from one with the literal meaning, 'strong in counsel'.

RHINE (sometimes pronounced REEN): a man-made channel for receiving water to drain the surrounding Somerset lowlands – see MOOR. The word is the same one that refers to the German river. Compare Old English RYNE, a flow, and German RONNE, a channel. Rhines are slowmoving watercourses, relatively narrow inland but widening to river-size near the sea. The term DITCH is often used to refer to small rhines, sometimes because the speaker is unaware of the difference between rhine and ditch, sometimes in the belief that the hearer (perhaps a 'voreigner') will not understand the meaning of RHINE. Also RHYNE. And see DITCH, DRAIN.

RHYNE: as RHINE.

RICK: a stack (of hay, etc). The use of the term is comparatively rare now that such stacks are comparatively rare.

RICK-BARTON: still occasionally used, referring to the farmyard where the ricks - see RICK - used to be, but are now rarely, kept.

RINDS: the removed skins of potatoes. See TATY.

RING: to castrate (lambs, young calves) by the application of a rubber ring. See CUT, PINCH.

Suckers (see page 53)

ROLLER: two (sometimes more) cuts or lines - see SWOTH - of hay put together in a row to facilitate drying and baling. Thus, ROLLER IT (or THEM) UP. Also RULLER, WAKE, WALL, WINDROW.

ROZZUM: a tall tale. "That's a b..... rozzum to tell I!" Also RUZZUM.

Ruckles/Tates (see below and page 55)

RUCKLE: in the peat industry, which is still substantial in Central Somerset, machines have taken over a great part of the work previously done by hand. But, where peat is still stacked by hand, the term RUCKLE may be used to refer to the process of making a certain form of stack for drying out the peat, and to the stack itself – a conical structure, looking rather like a beehive, nowadays usually made up to roughly five feet high. To this extent the term is now synonymous with TATE. In fact, in so far as any distinction is now made between the two, it is largely on the basis that a RUCKLE is 'filled' (has pieces of peat inside it) and that a TATE is hollow. See TATE, WALL, WINDROW. We have also come across RUCKLE meaning to crease. Compare Standard English RUCK.

RULLER: as ROLLER.

RUZZUM: as ROZZUM.

S

Bear in mind that **s** is often pronounced as **z**.

SCAD: a quick, sudden shower of rain. Also SKIT.

SCALP: with reference to the quarrying of stone, to SCALP is to clean out waste products from the primary (crushed) material. SCALPINGS are the waste product, generally a mix of small stones with sand, clay or grit. This material is very useful for making drive-ways, for example, and providing firm access to lowland fields.

SCALPINGS: see SCALP.

SCAMMISH: clumsy, awkward. Also CLUMBER-SOME, GAMMY.

SCAMMISH-HANDED: left-handed - also BACK-HANDED, CACK-HANDED, LEFT-HANDED, SCRAMMY-HANDED; clumsy or awkward with the hands - also BACK-HANDED, CACK-HANDED, CLUMBLEFISTED, GAMMY-HANDED, HO-MICKY, LEFT-HANDED, MUZZLE-HANDED, SCRAMMY-HANDED.

SCRABBLE: to hurry. "I've got a lot to do, I'm going to scrabble on."

SCRAMMED: numb with cold; very cold.

SCRAMMY-HANDED: left-handed – also BACK-HANDED, CACK-HANDED, LEFT-HANDED, SCAMMISH-HANDED; clumsy or awkward with the hands – also BACK-HANDED, CACK-HANDED, CLUMBLEFISTED, GAMMY-HANDED, HO-MICKY, LEFT-HANDED, MUZZLE-HANDED, SCAMMISH-HANDED.

SCRATCHINGS: scraps of meat remaining after fat has been rendered.

SCREWS: a generic term for rheumatism, sciatica, arthritis, lumbago and allied aches and pains. "I'm not too well, I got the screws."

SCRUMPY: traditional farmhouse cider, unique in character, and a drink for which Somerset is famous. It is worth noting that Elworthy, in his **West Somerset Word-Book**, 1888, lists SCRUMPLING as a small apple which never reaches perfection. Also, SCRUMP is a West Country word meaning to crunch. Possibly SCRUMPTIOUS is connected too. (Of course it now means delightful, delicious, for many an apt description of SCRUMPY; but one should bear in mind that it used to mean stingy.)

SCUTTY: the wren.

SHACKLE: to walk, go, get along. "I must shackle on home." Sometimes the notion of shambling or shuffling is involved.

SHAM: a (mechanised) hoe, an inter-row cultivator. The term was earlier used to refer to a horse-hoe.

SHARD: a gap or hole in a hedge or wall. Also SHERD.

SHAVE: to whittle, trim a stick. Also SKIN, STRIP.

SHAVINGS: chaff. Also CAVINGS, HUSKS. The word is also used of wood parings.

SHERD: as SHARD.

SHOOT: the guttering on a house. Also SHOOT-ING.

SHOOTING: as SHOOT.

A Drove (see page 20)

SHRIMP: a shoot on a potato. To SHRIMP a potato is to remove such shoots. But to SHRIMP is also used to refer to making do – compare Standard English SKIMP and SCRIMP.

SKIDS: a contraption consisting of two wooden poles held together by chains and used in the loading and unloading of barrels, for example barrels of cider. To SKID the barrels is to roll them down the skids, in other words to unload them. In loading barrels one ROLLS them up the skids.

SKIMMISHED: drunk. Also PUGGLED.

SKIN: to whittle, trim a stick. Also SHAVE, STRIP.

SKIT: as SCAD.

SLASHER: a long-handled implement with a heavy, curved blade, for cutting hedges, briars, 'rubbish', etc. See STAFFHOOK.

SLIP: a piglet; a young pig some seven or eight weeks old. Also SQUEALER. And see SUCKER.

SLURRY: 'waste' material, usually consisting of animal excrement, in liquid or semi-liquid form.

SMEECH: smoke; an unpleasant smell (usually of smoke); a sooty patch on a ceiling.

SNAG-PIPE: the great horse-tail, Equisetum Maximum, which looks somewhat like a small fir-tree. Poisonous to cattle and extremely difficult to get rid of. Also SNAKE-PIPE, TAB-PIPE, TAG-PIPE.

SNAKE-PIPE: as SNAG-PIPE.

SNO?: do you know? In other words, DOST KNOW? abbreviated.

SOMEWHEN: sometime. See ANYWHEN.

SOUR DOCK: sorrel, which has a sour taste.

SPARK: to make sparks, and to spit, as firewood may in a fire. So a fire may be SPARKING, an expression also used of courting, going courting. Of course sparks may well be made in both cases. See HOP.

SPECKLES: freckles or spots.

SPRAYED: chapped, one's hands or face sore or rough from cold or wind. Also SPREEVED.

SPREEVED: as SPRAYED.

SQUARE: solid, well-built. A SQUARE HOUSE is a big, more or less square-shaped house which is considered solid and well-built.

SQUAT: not only to sit down on the heels, etc - also QUAT - but to squash, squeeze.

SQUEAKER: the runt in a litter of pigs - also CADDY, CADMAN, CAGMAN, JOEY. It is also used of a mouse, and of a pheasant chick.

SQUEALER: a small pig. Also SLIP. And see SUCKER.

SQUIRE: a form of address, sometimes respectful or mildly flattering, sometimes jokey or even mildly sarcastic, to someone (male) in authority - see GAFFER - or someone who is considered, or considers himself, 'higher' in the social scale.

STAFFHOOK: a very long-handled implement with a long, rounded (C-shaped) blade. Used for lighter hedging, its work is now often done with a SLASHER (see above).

Steers

STEER (sometimes pronounced STIR or STUR): a bullock.

STEERED: castrated, of a bullock. See STEER.

STEWER: bad temper. "He's in a bit of a stewer." Also FADDY. STEWER is also used of sulking or moping, and a STEWER is one who sulks or mopes, to STEWER is to sulk or mope.

STICKING: fetching and, when necessary, cutting wood. Thus, TO GO STICKING.

STOOK: to stand several (or more) sheaves of corn or straw against each other for drying; a set of sheaves stacked in this way. The practice is outmoded now so far as grain is concerned, but it is still in existence where straw to be used for thatching is dried.

STRIP: to whittle, trim a stick. Also SHAVE, SKIN.

STUFFLE: to stifle - "You're trying to stuffle me"; to stuff with food.

SUCKER: a piglet, or any suckling animal. See SLIP, SQUEALER.

SWALLET-HOLE: holes, such as in the Mendips, into which streams disappear and go underground. These holes, getting larger and larger, may eventually cave in under the weight of some object and swallow it up.

SWEETHEARTS: goosegrass, which clings. Also CLIDER.

SWOTH: like Standard English SWATHE, a single cut or line of grass, hay, etc.

TAB-PIPE: the great horse-tail, Equisetum Maximum, which looks somewhat like a small fir-tree. Poisonous to cattle and extremely difficult to get rid of. Also TAG-PIPE, SNAG-PIPE, SNAKE-PIPE.

TACKER-WEED: knot grass, Polygonum Aviculare, a very common weed - TACKER from its likeness to shoemakers' (tough) waxed thread of that name.

TAG-PIPE: as TAB-PIPE.

TALLET: barn; loft.

TASTY: not used only of that which has a good taste, but also to refer to mature cheddar cheese, which (usually) has a 'strong' taste. "Have you got any tasty?"

TATE: in the peat industry, which is still substantial in Central Somerset, machines have taken over a great part of the work previously done by hand. But, where peat is still stacked by hand, the term TATE may be used to refer to the process of making a certain form of stack for drying out the peat, and to the stack itself - a conical structure, looking rather like a beehive, made to a height of up to roughly five feet. To this extent the term is now synonymous with RUCKLE. In fact, in so far as any distinction is now made between the two, it is largely on the basis that a TATE is hollow and a RUCKLE 'filled', i.e. has pieces of peat inside it. See RUCKLE, WALL, WINDROW.

TATY: potato. TATY-RINDS are potato skins, a TATY-TRAP is a mouth. Also CHEDDY, CHITTY, TEDDY, TIDDY.

TEART: tender or sore (as of a cut or blister); also of soil and pastureland deficient in copper. A form of TART.

TED: to fluff up and spread rows of hay to help in drying it. A TEDDER is a machine for doing this, now superseded by a Woofler - see WOOFLER.

TEDDY: potato. Also CHEDDY, CHITTY, TATY, TIDDY.

THIK: that; this.

TIDDY: as TEDDY.

TOLL: to help something down, as with jam on bread; to entice or lure (for example, a pheasant). In other words to attract or make attractive.

TOMMY: food, especially when taken to work; a loaf of bread.

TOR: Common in South Western place names, it refers to a hill or high rock. So, in GLASTONBURY TOR, it refers to the hill and not to the tower on the top of it. From Old English TORR, a rock, a rocky outcrop, a rocky peak, and going back to a root with the meaning bulge, belly. Thus, applied to the landscape, a bulging hill.

TORMENT: to tease, annoy, badger.

TOWSE: to give a playful smack on the head, as to a child or puppy.

TRIG: to prop up.

TRUCKLE: a whole cheese (small or large) of a truckle shape – that is, the shape of a wheel or castor, which is also a TRUCKLE as in TRUCKLE-BED. Thus other things of similar shape, such as sheep's dung – see TRUCKLES, below – may be known by the same name. In the case of whole cheeses, which are often very large and heavy, this shape enables them to be moved more readily by rolling them.

TRUCKLES: the word is used to refer to both the 'bound' heaps of dung such as sheep's and to the 'loose' droppings. See CURRANTS, TRUCKLE.

TUNDISH: a funnel for pouring liquids into a container. Also TUNNIGER.

TUNNIGER: as TUNDISH.

TURDSTOOL: a patch of cow-dung, a cowpat.

TURMET: a turnip. TURNIP distorted.

U

UPALONG: along, towards, or near - all in a generally upward direction from where one is. See DOWNALONG.

URGE: to vomit - "That made I urge"; to try to vomit.

A Drain (see page 20)

V

VERDIC: opinion, viewpoint. "Well, that's my verdic." Compare Standard English VERDICT.

VINNY: sour; mouldy. But, used of cheese, as in BLUE VINNY, the word simply refers to the blue mould which runs through the cheese. This type of mould is deliberately introduced to 'blue' the cheese.

VIPER: an adder (ADDER is also used) or – as in common usage – venomous snakes generally. See HARRY.

VOREIGNER: foreigner. Such a pronunciation might well cause confusion. At any rate, VOREIGNER or FOREIGNER mean, essentially, anyone born outside 'old' Somerset. "If werr's'nt born in Zummerzet, / thee'rt a 'voreigner' to we", as Ray Burrows points out in his entertaining "They danged 'voreigners'", in his **Bide awhile wi' I: Somerset Dialect Poems**, 1980. However, a residence of, say, twenty and more years evidently makes one less 'voreign' than one was, and certainly not a holiday maker or tourist – see GROCKLE.

W

WAKE: two (sometimes more) cuts or lines - see SWOTH - of hay put together to facilitate drying and baling. To WAKE IT (or THEM) UP is, in this context, to consolidate the lines for this purpose. Also ROLLER, RULLER, WALL, WINDROW.

WALL: in farming, the term is used to refer to two (sometimes more) cuts or lines - see SWOTH - of hay put together to facilitate drying and baling. To WALL IT (or THEM) UP is to do this. Also ROLLER, RULLER, WAKE, WINDROW. The term is also used in the peat industry to refer to long, straight rows, roughly three feet high, of peat spits (with or without spaces in between them - see WINDROW) usually, though not invariably, stacked by machine. In fact peat is now very largely stacked in this way. See RUCKLE, TATE.

WANT: a mole. So a WANT-HEAP is a mole-hill, a WANT-WRIGGLE is a mole-track. To SHINE LIKE A WANT is to shine or glow like a (sleek furred) mole. To go WANTING is to go hunting moles, animals which can do considerable damage to crops, lawns, etc. Also WONT.

WICKERING: the neighing or whinnying of a horse; the whining of a dog.

WHILE: until. "I'll be here while half ten."

WINDBAG: a gossip. Also CHAMMER, CHATTER-BAG, NAGGAR, NEWSBAG, RAGBAG. WINDBAG is also used to refer to a boastful person.

WINDROW: two (sometimes more) cuts or lines of hay – see SWOTH – put together to facilitate drying and baling. To WINDROW is, in this context, to consolidate the lines for this purpose. Or the process may be referred to as ROWING THEM (or IT) UP. Also ROLLER, RULLER, WAKE, WALL. The term is also still used occasionally to refer to the process of making a certain form of stack for drying out peat, and to the stack itself – two rows, some three feet high and three feet apart, of spits spaced out in a kind of lattice-work design. But such stacks are now more often referred to as WALLS – see WALL – a term also used to refer to stacks which have not been spaced in this way. See RUCKLE, TATE.

WISP: a stye, a pustule at the margin of the eyelid. STYE is now commoner.

WITHY: a willow tree or osier. WITHIES are not only a familiar and lovely element of the landscape, they are grown for use in such crafts as basket-making.

WITHYWIND (often pronounced WIDDYWINE): bindweed, Convolvulus Arvensis. WITHY because its root and stem resemble the willow tree and osiers in their toughness and flexibility, WIND because it winds or twines round any possible support.

WONT: as WANT.

WOOD QUIST: a wood pigeon. Also just QUIST. But the expression is now thought of as 'old'.

WOOFLER: a machine for fluffing up and spreading rows of hay to help in drying it. To WOOFLE is what the machine does. See TED.

WOOZEY-MINDED: absent-minded; malicious; bloody-minded.

WOPS: a wasp. Also WOPSY.

WOPSY: as WOPS.

Cheese (see page 13)

Y

YEAR-GRASS: grass that grows after the cut made for hay. Also AFTERCUT, AFTERGRASS, HE-GRASS.

YOP: like YAP, to talk alot. A YOPPER is a big talker, a loquacious individual. Also CHAMMER.

Withywind (see page 60)

Z

ZACKLY: exactly; and, with a negative, meaning not quite all there, half-witted. "Well, he isn't zackly..." (Compare the slang expressions still in use, TO BE A BUTTON SHORT, TO HAVE LOST A BUTTON, meaning slightly crazy, a bit dim.)

Moors in Flood (see page 35)

FURTHER READING

BROOK, G.L., English Dialects, 1963 (1965).

ORTON, H. et al, Survey of English Dialects, 1962-70.

ORTON, H and WRIGHT, N., A Word Geography of England, 1974.

PHILLIPPS, K.C., Westcountry Words and Ways, 1976.

QUIRK, R., The Use of English, 1962 (1968).

ROGERS, N., Wessex Dialect, 1979.

WAKELIN, M.F., English Dialects: An Introduction, 1972 (1977).

WARBURG, J.F., Verbal Values, 1966.